Copyright: Rawda Press 2016 (Imprint of IDEA Press)
ISBN: 978-0-9929736-3-6

Published by:
Rawda Press
62 Church Road
London E12 6AF
0207 998 7768

Title: **Life of Muhammad the Sublime**
                - Biography Simply Told in Poetic Rhyme

Author: **Moin Uddin Khan**

Published by: **Rawda Press 2016** (Imprint of IDEA Press)

Cover Design: **Moin Uddin Khan**

Printed by: **Mega Printers, Turkey**

بسم الله الرحمن الرحيم

LIFE OF

MUHAMMAD THE SUBLIME

BIOGRAPHY SIMPLY TOLD IN POETIC RHYME

LIFE OF
MUHAMMAD THE SUBLIME
BIOGRAPHY SIMPLY TOLD IN POETIC RHYME

MOIN UDDIN KHAN

Dedication

Dedicated to my teachers and my ultimate source of
inspiration, in whose company I yearn to be in.

Contents

Author's Note

اَلسَّـــلَامُ عَلَيْكُمْ وَرَحْمَةُ اللّهِ وَبَرَكَاتُهُ

All praise is due to Allah, Lord of the worlds, we praise
him and seek his aid and we send salutations upon his
beloved messenger Muhammad, the chosen one, peace and
blessings of Allah be upon him and his family, companions
and all those who follow them in guidance.

A few years ago this feeble servant took upon himself
to write the biography of the best of creation in a simple,
creative and enjoyable text, which would allow access for
everyone from children, adults, scholars and laity to read,
learn and easily teach the life of the messenger of Allah .
Though there are numerous biographies on the
Messenger , most are very in-depth, detailed and lengthy.
I wanted to write something which would be short, concise
and in a chronological order, whilst being enjoyable to read
due to the simple poetic rhyming nature of the book.
Alhamdulilah this is the humble work you find here. I have
named it 'Life of Muhammad the Sublime, Biography
Simply Told in Poetic Rhyme'.
I have kept the book in the spirit of the *sunnah* and the
established traditions and not delved into too much detail
of issues where there is genuine difference.
This work can be used as an informative read as well as
a *matn*/source text for the teaching of the *seerah*, allowing
individual teachers to give their own explanations to
supplement this text *inshaAllah*.

Moin Uddin Khan
Shaban 1437 / May 2016

IBRAHIM'S ﷺ PRAYER

Inspired by Allah; Ibrahim ﷺ travelled to Arabia with his son and spouse.

He said "O our Lord, I leave my offspring next to your sacred house.

Our Lord, I leave them in a valley that is barren and bare.

Our Lord, make them of those who establish prayer.

Incline people's hearts towards them to treat them with care.

Our Lord, fulfil their needs and provide them with fruits.

So that they may be of those who show gratitude. [1]

Our Lord, make us into people who turn to you in submission.

And grant from our offspring a submissive nation. [2]

Our Lord, send to them a messenger from amongst them.

Who will recite your verses, teach them your book and wisdom.

And one who will be a means for their purification." [3]

Allah accepted this prayer of his and took Ibrahim✳ as a friend.

And from his progeny through Ismail✳ was to come the best of all men.

1   *Ibrahim, verse 37, Al Qur'an*
2   *Al Baqara, verse 128, Al Qur'an*
3   *Al Baqara, verse 129, Al Qur'an*

YEAR OF THE ELEPHANT

The Arabs had a tradition of remembering dates
by their events.

Muhammad ﷺ was born on a Monday in Rabiul
Awwal in the year of the elephant. [4]

When Allah most high was able to prevent
Abraha and his army from their evil intent.

They wanted to destroy the Kabah which
Ibrahim ﷺ had built. [5]

But when the army drew close their elephants
stood still.

Allah caused birds to fly over the army
in flocks.

Striking them with stones made of baked clay
and rocks. [6]

Though the army was destroyed and Allah's
house was saved.

The Kabah was still in the hands of those who
were astray.

It housed over 300 idols, different ones worshipped on different days.

They had many gods: gods of food, wealth, clan and place.

Arabia had many tribes; the best of them was Quraish.

Quraish were in charge of the annual Hajj, they were known for their trade.

They would travel all summer and winter. Allah would provide for them and keep them safe. [7]

4   *Ibn Hisham & Jami' Al Tirmizi, book of virtues*
5   *Al Baqara, verse 127, Al Qur'an*
6   *Al Fil, Al Qur'an*
7   *Al Quraish, Al Qur'an*

BIRTH AND CHILDHOOD

His father Abdullah was of Bani Hashim, a clan from the Quraishi tribe.

His father passed away whilst his mother Amina was just a new bride. [8]

From his first moment into this world, he started life as an orphan.

He was to be sent to live with the bedouins as was the Arab custom.

Halima came to the city to take an infant as she was a wet nurse.

The wet nurses were eager to get to the rich families first.

From this orphan, she felt she would not get her efforts worth. [9]

But taking the baby home brought unexpected blessings into her household.

No sooner as she placed him onto her lap, her milk started to overflow.

He stayed with her family in the desert until the age of four.

One day Muhammadﷺ was outside with other children at play.

Two angels came and made him lay, they opened up his chest and washed his heart in a tray. [10]

They removed a dark clot that causes sin, and left him looking pale and grey.

Muhammadﷺ was quickly returned to stay at his mother's side.

After two years, suddenly Amina fell ill on a journey and in her illness she died.

He was taken under the care of his grandfather, to whom he was very dear.

His sadness was great at the death of his grandfather after staying there for two years.

8 Ibn Hisham, vol.1 page 120
9 Ibn Hisham, vol.1 page 123
10 Sahih Muslim, book of faith

GROWING UP AND TRAVELS

Muhammad ﷺ went to live with his uncle Abu Talib and his family.

Abu Talib was not a rich man, so Muhammad ﷺ would work to help financially.

He would serve as a shepherd, and would join their business travels occasionally. [11]

Once they were passing a monastery, on their journey to Syria for trade.

A monk noticed that the clouds would follow him and trees would move to give him shade.

He invited them for food and saw the seal of the prophets between his shoulder blades.

The monk said "He is the mercy to mankind, the chief of the messengers.

I have been waiting for his arrival, it is written in the scriptures." [12]

He advised Abu Talib not to take Muhammad ﷺ any further.

If some Romans or Jews were to recognise him his life would be in danger.

As Muhammadﷺ matured, he became a professional merchant.

Khadija a rich woman hired him and sent him on business with her servant. [13]

Since employing Muhammad,ﷺ Khadija saw her profits rise.

On hearing about his noble character, she proposed to be his wife.

Muhammadﷺ agreed, and he married Khadija at the age of twenty five.

Allah blessed them with many children, and they had a happy marital life.

11   Sahih Al Bukhari, book of hiring
12   Jami' Al Tirmizi, book of virtues
13   Ibn Hisham, vol.1 page 141

PRE-PROPHETHOOD

The people of Makkah decided to rebuild the Kabah as it was damaged due to flood.

Everyone was able to contribute but only pure money would enter the fund. [14]

A dispute arose on placing back the blackstone, one would not allow the other leading to a grudge.

They decided that the next person to walk in through the gates would be the judge.

When Muhammadﷺ walked in they said, "It is Al Amin! He is a person who everyone trusts."

He advised the blackstone be placed on a cloth, each corner for every leader to clutch.

He pushed the blackstone into place himself, using wisdom to prevent the shedding of blood. [15]

Muhammadﷺ had a reputation as an honest man and all would treat him with respect.

And he would join pacts like 'hilf al fudhul' to help the weak who were being oppressed. [16]

As he approached the age of forty, Muhammad ﷺ constantly felt an internal unrest.

He would ponder over the state of the people and had thoughts he could not express.

He would see dreams clear as daylight, in his mind the vision remained fresh.

Unable to explain to anyone he would seek solitude to reflect.

14   *Ibn Hisham, vol.1 page 144*
15   *Ibn Hisham, vol.1 page 146*
16   *Adab Al Mufrad, book of behaviour*

FIRST REVELATION

Muhammadﷺ preferred to spend time in a cave called Hira, where he would contemplate. [17]

When he was at the age of forty, he was sitting in the cave wide awake.

The Angel Jibreelﷺ came to him and said, "Read." He replied truthfully, "I cannot read."

The Angel then took hold of him and pressed him until he felt squeezed.

The Angel released him and repeated, "Read." He replied the second time, "I cannot read."

The Angel pressed him again, this happened thrice until he felt his breathing would stop.

Releasing him he said, "Read in the name of your Lord who created, created man from a clot.

Read, & your Lord is most gracious, who taught by the pen, taught man what he knew not." [18]

Muhammadﷺ returned home trembling and said, "Cover me, cover me," to his wife.

He informed his wife Khadija of the event and said how he feared for his life.

"No! Allah would not disgrace you," she said, "You speak the truth, and maintain family ties."

Khadija took her husband to her cousin Waraqa ibn Nawfal to seek his advice.

He was a Christian who had studied the scriptures; now old and lost the sight in his eyes. [19]

"This was the same Angel who came to Musa," he said, "You are a Prophet to this nation.

You will be expelled by your people, all who came before you also faced persecution."

Waraqa added, "If I live to see that day then I will stand by you till the end."

The first to believe in the prophet was Khadija, and his cousin Ali who was a youth of ten. [20]

Also Abu Bakr his close companion followed by other family and friends.

17   Sahih Al Bukhari, book of revelation
18   Al Alaq, verses 1-5, Al Qur'an
19   Sahih Al Bukhari, book of revelation
20   Ibn Hisham, vol.1 page 178

OPEN PROCLAMATION

For the first three years after revelation, secretly
Muhammadﷺ would preach.

Mostly the poor had accepted the message and only
a handful from the elite.

Now Allah commanded his prophet; openly the
message is to be declared.

Muhammadﷺ ascended mount Safa and cried out,
"O people of Quraish: beware! [21]

If I was to say some horsemen are advancing to
attack you, would you trust me?"

They replied "Certainly, we have always found you
to be trustworthy."

He said, "I am a warner to you before a severe
torment, so fear Allah and follow me."

The Quraish were shocked and silent, only Abu
Lahab responded with curse.

Regarding whom Allah revealed, "May the hands of
Abu Lahab perish," in a Quranic verse. [22]

Muhammadﷺ would now preach to everyone and at Darul Arqam they would meet.

The Quraish would threaten the new Muslims and the poor ones they would beat.

They tried to bribe the Prophet, saying "We will give you all the wealth you seek.

We will marry you to the most beautiful women and will make you our leader and chief."

Muhammadﷺ said, "If they were to put the sun on my right hand and the moon on my left.

And they ask me to abandon this call; I would not turn from it until victory or my death." [23]

The Prophetﷺ advised the weaker Muslims; to Abyssinia they should migrate.

It was the land of a righteous King, in whose court oppressors cannot dictate.

The Muslims left for Abyssinia quietly, led by Uthman and the Prophet's daughter Ruqayya. [24]

The Quraish tried to intercept them but lost track of them in the deserts of Arabia.

---

21   *Sahih Muslim, book of faith*
22   *Al Masad, verse 1, Al Qur'an*
23   *Ibn Hisham, vol.1 page 206*
24   *Ibn Hisham, vol.1 page 227*

THE YEARS OF SORROW

The Quraish would tell people "He is a sorcerer,"
but still his message they could not stop.

The Prophet's clan would not hand him over, so
they decreed upon them a social boycott.

Bani Hashim moved out of Makkah and had to live
in a narrow mountain pass.

Three years under siege, when food was short they
would resort to eating grass.

The siege was ended when termites destroyed the
agreement except for Allah's name. [25]

Though Bani Hashim were now free, the boycott
already had its strain.

Soon after returning to Makkah, came the death of
Abu Talib, his uncle and tribal protector.

Situation got even worse, as he lost his wife Khadija;
the believing people's mother.

Her loss was great on him as she was his advisor
and emotional supporter.

The Makkans would now openly campaign against the Muslims with torture.

The Prophetﷺ would speak to pilgrims to negotiate an alliance with a tribe.

A place where believers can practice freely without fearing for their lives.

TAIF

The Prophet ﷺ decided to travel to Taif, he walked there with Zayd: his adopted son.

He called the leaders to the oneness of God, but wherever he went he was shunned.

The people stirred the children against the Prophet, pelting him with stones for fun.

The street was full with people attacking him, Zayd tried to cover the blows.

He walked out of Taif with tears in his eyes, blood dripping from head to toes.

They sought refuge next to a wall, Muhammad ﷺ raised his hands to express his sorrows.

He supplicated . . .

*"O My Lord! only to you I complain for my
weakness in ability.*

*And my humiliation in front of the people, you are the
best of those who show mercy.*

*You are my Lord and the Lord of the weak.
To whom have you entrusted me?*

*Have you entrusted me to those who wish ill?
or put me in the care of my enemies?*

*I am not worried so long as you are not angry with me,
for your favours are abundant for me.*

*I seek refuge in the light of you countenance
by which all darkness is enlightened.*

*By the means of which all matters of this world
and the next world are rightened.*

*I seek refuge lest your anger descends upon me
or your displeasure.*

*I desire your satisfaction in me and your felicity,
besides you there is no might nor power."*

Two angels came and said, "If you choose, we will destroy people of Taif between these two hills."

He replied, "Perhaps people will come from their progeny who will believe, if Allah wills." [26]

Thinking about his options before returning, the Prophet ﷺ decided to stay there the night.

A group of Jinns who overheard him reading the Qur'an, they said, "Listen to what he recites.

O our people, we heard a book revealed after Musa, ﷺ the books before it, it verifies.

It guides to the truth and guides towards the path that is right.

O our people, answer the call of the Prophet, ﷺ that with your Lord none should be ascribed." [27]

26   *Al Bukhari, book of beginning of creation*
27   *Al Jinn, verses 1-2 & Al Ahqaf verses 29-31, Al Qur'an*

NIGHT JOURNEY & ASCENSION

One night a few angels including Jibreel came and woke Muhammad from his sleep.

They brought with them the Buraq, a mount bigger than a donkey but smaller than a steed. [28]

They rode it from Masjidul Haram to Masjidul Aqsa in Jerusalem at magnificent speed.

They found many prophets waiting to pray, Jibreel took Muhammad forward to lead.

He led two rakat salah, behind him was every single prophet born from Adam's seed.

Confirming that he is the seal of the prophets, whom no other prophet would succeed. [29]

From there on they ascended to the gates of the first heaven where Jibreel sought entry.

One by one they passed the seven heavens until they reached the furthest Lote tree.

Jibreel had to stop here, Muhammad continued until he came to the divine proximity. [30]

Allah gifted five times salah to the Muslim nation, the reward for which would be fifty. [31]

The Prophetﷺ was returned to his home in Makkah and it was as if he had just left.

The people of Makkah took this opportunity to make his experience into jest.

But he informed them of approaching caravans and describing Jerusalem in depth.

Even many Muslims were shocked by this incident, but Abu Bakr was first to attest. [32]

28   Al Isra', verse 1, Al Qur'an
29   Ibn Hisham, vol.1 page 285
30   Referred to in Al Najm, verses 8-18, Al Qur'an
31   Al Bukhari, book of beginning of creation
32   Ibn Hisham, vol.1 page 287

THE MIGRATION

Some pilgrims from Yathrib embraced Islam and to
their city they wanted to invite.

They wanted the Prophetﷺ to become their leader
and to stop their tribal strife.

Perhaps through accepting Islam Allah would cause
their hearts to unite.

The Prophetﷺ said "I take your pledge, that you
protect me like your womenfolk."

"In return yours will be paradise and for your
blessing and unity I will invoke." [33]

The Prophet gave permission for the Muslims to
migrate to the new Muslim state.

The pagans were monitoring the Prophet's house,
but he was able to escape.

Their plot was to kill the Prophet, but Allah blinded
them with dust in their face.

They went into his house at night, but they found
Ali had taken his place. [34]

Abu Bakr and the Prophet set off on their journey with the pagans giving chase.

To lose track of them, they hid for a few days in a mountain cave.

Allah was the third of them, who used a spider's web to hinder the pagan's gaze. [35]

They sought the help of a bedouin to guide via a remote route along the coast.

Along the journey they requested a women if she would be their host.

She was Um Ma'bad, she said, "I have no food nor milk, just this sickly goat."

The Prophet's blessed hands milked it until the container filled to the topmost.

They drank to their full and continued on their journey along the dusty road.

When Um Ma'bad's husband returned, she described the Prophet in the best way told . . . [36]

"

He was a man who was handsome,
with a glowing countenance.

He was of good proportion,
neither a small head nor large abdomen.

He was of smart appearance,
he had deep black eyes and long eye lashes.

He had well balanced features,
his voice was not coarse nor harsh.

He had a long neck and a full round beard.

He had thick eyebrows, in the middle they paired.

When he was silent, he was deliberate and composed.

His expressions were august whenever he spoke.

He was well spoken, distinguished in utterance.

Talking neither excessively, nor was the message insufficient.

His words flowing like a perfect string of pearls.

He was neither short nor overly tall.

A noble man in the company of other nobles.

He was well served, though he was not stern nor dictatorial.

"

33   *Ibn Hisham, vol.1 page 313*
34   *Ibn Hisham, vol.1 page 352*
35   *Al Tawba, verse 40, Al Qur'an*
36   *Zad al Ma'ad,vol 2, page 50*

THE CITY OF THE PROPHET

On a Monday 14 years after prophethood, the
Prophetﷺ reached Quba in the outskirts of the city.

In Quba he laid the base of a masjid, the foundation
of which was piety.

After a few days the Prophetﷺ left for Yathrib on
his camel, where all the Muslims awaited.

The men came out in armour to greet them, girls
sang songs and the whole city celebrated.

Many people would offer, "O prophet, honour us
by staying with us as our guest."

He replied "Let this camel move freely, I will stay
wherever she sits to rest."

Allah guided the camel to stop where it did, this is
where the masjid of the Prophetﷺ was built. 37

A room was made for the Prophetﷺ next door, a
simple structure from mud and grit.

The Ansar welcomed the migrating Muslims who
left behind their families, homes and wealth.

The climate of Yathrib did not suit the newcomers,
they were soon homesick due to ill health.

The Prophetﷺ supplicated, "O Allah, make us love
this city like we loved Makkah but at an increase.

Bless the agriculture here, bless its transactions and
remove from it its disease."[38]

In honour of the Prophet'sﷺ arrival, Yathrib was
renamed Madina, 'The Illuminated City'.

Madina had a big population of Jews and Pagans,
the Muslims signed with them a treaty,

That the three parties would support each other and
live peacefully as a community.

Allah told the Muslims to change their qibla from
Jerusalem to Makkah, to which there were critics.

A new challenge the believers were now facing was
that amongst them were now hypocrites.

37   Ibn Hisham, vol.1 page 364
38   Sahih Al Bukhari, book of patients

THE BATTLE OF BADR

The Quraish seized all the Muslim's property, their families in Makkah had no rights.

Two years after Hijra, Allah gave the believers permission to defend their properties and lives.

"Permission to fight has been given to those who are oppressed and expelled from their homes." [39]

The Prophetﷺ wanted to raid a Quraishi caravan as a warning to leave the Muslims alone.

The Makkans assembled an army of over 1000 strong, as the Muslim plan became known.

The Prophetﷺ sought the Ansar's counsel, they said "Fight! We will not leave you on your own." [40]

The Quraish came to the battlefield and challenged three Muslims to a duelling war.

Ali, Hamza and Ubaidah faced them to the duel and all three were victors.

The battle started with the Muslims outnumbered against a much larger force.

Inspired by their Prophet, 313 believers fought equipped with spears and swords.

Allah reinforced them with angels descending in succession led by Jibreel﷽ on his horse. [41]

They fought with courage whilst the pagans fled the field after facing a heavily loss.

Thus Allah caused the truth to prevail and conquer over that which was false.

39   *Al Haj, verses 39-40 Al Qur'an*
40   *Ibn Hisham, vol.1 page 458*
41   *Al Anfal, verse 8, Al Qur'an*

THE BATTLE OF UHUD

The Makkans were humiliated at Badr and now they sought revenge.

They rallied their allies and neighbouring tribes to gather over 3000 men.

The Prophet ﷺ wanted to remain in the city so that all could take part in defence.

Muslims who missed Badr were eager to go and face the enemies seeking honour.

The Prophet ﷺ accepted and came out prepared wearing two layers of armour.

On the way to battle 300 of the cavalry abandoned the army showing their true colours.

With only 700 soldiers, the Prophet appointed a small hill to be used to host 50 archers.

He ﷺ ordered, "Stay in your positions even if our bodies are being eaten by vultures." [42]

The battle raged on with the Muslims outnumbered by four times the troops.

Many sahabas were martyred and the Prophetﷺ was wounded and lost a tooth. [43]

The believers fought valiantly causing some pagans to flee with Muslims in pursuit.

Thinking the Muslims had won, most of the archers moved to gather the loot.

Khalid ibn Walid noticed this and attacked the Muslims from behind using an alternative route.

The believers were surrounded so they climbed up mount Uhud to escape.

The pagans were unable to reach them but any dead they found they would mutilate.

The Muslims declared, "Our dead are in paradise, for your dead a torment awaits."

42   Sahih Al Bukhari, book of Jihad
43   Jami' Al Tirmizi, book of Tafsir

THE BATTLE OF THE TRENCH

The Prophet would send his companions as peaceful delegation to other tribes.

They would go to teach the message but due to treachery many companions died.

Jews of Banu Nazir in Madina tried to kill the Prophet thus breaking the alliance pact.

They were laid siege to for their treachery and their gardens were hacked.

After six days they surrendered and left with their belongings never to come back.

Now the hypocrites, the Jews and the pagans became allies and common friends.

They united against the Muslims with Arabia's biggest military offence.

The Prophet consulted the companions as to which was the best means of defence.

Salman the Persian advised the city to be secured by digging a trench.

The army wanted to attack but were unable to breach the city.

News came that Jews of Bani Quraiza had decided to break the treaty.

The Prophetﷺ feared for the women and children as they now faced internal hostility.

The coalition laid siege to Madina, but Allah instilled within them disunity.

A storm raged their camp for many days and the cold was affecting them brutally.

The pagans decided to abandon the siege and returned back to their community.

The Muslims did not sheathe their swords until they dealt with the internal threat.

They laid siege to Bani Quraiza who surrendered so long as their conditions were met.

They wanted their previous ally Sa'd ibn Mu'az from Al Aws to be the judge and to arbitrate.

Sa'd decreed that the punishment written in the Torah for treason, that should be their fate. [44]

44   *Can be found in the Bible, Deuteronomy 20.11 to 20.15*

THE TREATY OF HUDAIBIYA

After many years of conflict, Madina had now
become an established state.

Realising the Muslims could not be defeated,
they opted to character assassinate.

The hypocrites spread rumours about Aisha the
Mother of the Believers.

Madina was in complete shock until Allah cleared
her name by revealing a verse. [45]

The Prophetﷺ had a dream where he saw the
Muslims in Makkah fulfilling the pilgrim's rites.

Over 1400 Muslims prepared for the Umrah journey
without any intentions to fight.

They entered into the state of ihram and took with
them their animals for sacrifice.

They drew close to the city of Makkah and at
Hudaibiya they made their campsite.

The Prophetﷺ sent Uthman ibn Affan to speak to
the Quraish as he had protection from his clan.

News ___ ___ an's death, the Prophetﷺ summoned ___ ___ ake a stand.

They pledged to aveng ___ hman's death, one by one all of them placed th ___ hands.

"Allah was pleased with t ___ believers when they offered their allegiance un ___ the tree.

As Allah knew what was ___ hin their hearts thus He sent down upon them ___ nquillity.

Soon to acquire much sp ___ s of war and He would reward them with an i ___ nent victory." [46]

Uthman was found to ___ safe and the Quraish were willing to negotiate a ___ ace treaty.

That the Muslims ___ ld turn back now and could return for Umrah ___ next year.

Th ___ re woul ___ years of truce where the ___ ___ ite the Arabs without fear.

___ ___ ﷺ agreed and he was the first to ___ acrific ___ s animal and to cut his hair.

46 ___ 11 & 12, Al Qur'an
___ erses 18 & 19, Al Qur'an

INVITATION TO THE WORLD

The Prophet ﷺ sent messengers with invitation to
Islam to the leaders and kings.

In the name of Allah the most gracious the most
merciful it begins.

"From Muhammad the messenger of God to
Heraclius the great king of Rome.

I bear witness that there is none worthy of worship
except Allah alone.

Blessed are those who follow guidance, embrace
Islam and your sins will be atoned.

If you refuse then you would bear your follower's
sins as well as your own." [47]

Due to the peace with Quraish, people embraced
Islam in multitudes.

Everyday convoys would come to accept Islam from
the pagans and even the Jews.

But there was still hostility with some tribes like
Khaibar who had a feud.

The Muslims attacked their settlements and many small battles ensued.

Their fortresses were laid siege to, gaining for the Muslims much wealth and food.

They surrendered to be exiled with their belongings thus they were given a safe route.

The Prophetﷺ sent a letter to the King of Busra but he killed the messenger.

The Prophetﷺ was enraged and he sent an army of 3000 led by Zayd ibn Haritha.

Heﷺ said, "If Zayd is killed then appoint Jafar, if he is killed then Abdullah ibn Rawaha." [48]

They faced a huge Byzantine army at what was remembered as the Battle of Mu'tah.

All 3 of the Muslim leaders were slain, and then Khalid took the banner and took the lead.

He confused the Byzantine into thinking reinforcements came thus causing them to retreat.

He became known as 'Sword of Allah' and was able to prevent the Muslims from suffering a defeat.

47   Sahih Al Bukhari, book of Tafseer
48   Sahih Al Bukhari, book of Maghazi

CONQUEST OF MAKKAH

The Quraish supported another tribe to attack the Muslim's ally thus violating the truce.

The Quraish were offered to rectify the matter but out of pride they refused.

During the period of peace the Muslim population had heavily accrued.

Makkah was a sacred place, but the Muslim's battle for Makkah was now approved.

The Prophetﷺ left Madina with his companions and leading 10,000 troops.

They camped outside Makkah and different campfires were lit for every single group.

Abu Sufian was amazed at the sight of the army and could no longer deny the truth.

"All who are in Abu Sufian's house or their own homes will not be pursued."

The Prophetﷺ entered his birth city with his head lowered in humbleness and gratitude.

"The truth has come and falsehood has vanished, surely falsehood is bound to be removed." [49]

The Prophetﷺ said "Have no fear this day, besides a few criminals, all of you are excused."

The Quraish repented for their past and pledged their allegiance to Islam in multitudes.

Some tribes rallied against the Muslims bringing with them their wealth, children and women.

The Muslim army was 12,000, they felt that with such numbers victory was certain.

The two armies faced each other and a heavy battle raged in the valley of Hunain.

The Muslims faced such a force that many weaker Muslims fled whilst others were slain.

They forgot that victory is not by numbers, and that only happens what Allah has ordained.

The Prophetﷺ was almost alone, only a handful of companions remained.

Allah sent down tranquillity upon the believers and the Muslims were able to regain. [50]

They were victorious only with Allah's help, and much booty was gained.

The Prophetﷺ gave extra gifts to the new Muslims of Quraish to strengthen their faith.

Some Ansar felt now that Makkah was taken that the Prophetﷺ would want to stay.

The Prophetﷺ said "If the Ansar walk along a valley and all the people walk another way.

I would walk with the Ansar. All people are like outer clothes and Ansar are like inner garments.

O Ansar, are you not satisfied that whilst people return with cattle, you return with the Prophet?" [51]

49   Sahih Muslim, book of Jihad & Expeditions
50   Al Tawba, verse 25 7 26, Al Qur'an
51   Sahih Al Bukhari, Book of Maghazi

FAREWELL PILGRIMAGE

After the conquest of Makkah, one by one the tribes of Arabia came to accept faith.

The power of Islam quickly reached most of the peninsula at an amazing rate.

Ten years after Hijra the Prophet announced his intention to perform the pilgrimage.

Almost 100,000 Muslims joined him to learn the Hajj under his tutelage.

"Here I come answering your call my Lord, there is none like you, your call I answer.

Surely all praise, grace and dominion belongs to you, you have no partner."

At Arafat the prophetﷺ gave a sermon, "O people, listen to me, I may not be with you much longer.

Like this day, this month and this city; sacred is your blood, your property and your honour. [52]

No arab is better than a non-arab, nor is a white man better than one of a different colour.

I leave behind something, if you hold on to it you will not go astray; it is the book of Allah.

Inform others, perhaps the listener understands the message better than the informer.

O my people, what would you say when asked on the day of judgement; did I deliver?"

They said "You have delivered," he said, "O Allah be a witness in this matter."

The verse was revealed, "Today I have perfected your religion and completed upon you my favour."[53]

52   *Sunan ibn Majah, book of Rituals*
53   *Al Ma'idah, verse 3, Al Qur'an*

DEMISE OF THE MESSENGER

The Prophetﷺ returned to Madina, he was now at the age of sixty three.

One day he became very ill that he could not pray in the masjid so he asked Abu Bakr to lead.

He donated all his wealth and property as the prophets do not bequeath.

He advised, "You will never go astray as long as you grasp two things that I leave.

They are the Qur'an and my Sunnah, grasp them with your molar teeth."

The Prophetﷺ was unconscious for days and his pain gradually increased.

The day came when the light of this world disappeared and his soul had to leave.

The whole of Madina and every living thing in world was in a state of grief.

Many sahabas rejected the news and were in utter shock and disbelief.

Abu Bakr announced, "Whoever worshipped
Muhammad, know that Muhammad is deceased.

But whoever worships Allah, know that Allah is
ever living and does not cease.

Muhammad is only a messenger, many messengers
died before him in the past.

If he dies or is killed, are you going to turn
from the path?

Whoever turns will never harm Allah, surely to the
grateful ones Allah will grant." [54]

A dispute arose who should succeed the Prophetﷺ
to rule the Muslim lands.

Umar led the companions and gave his allegiance at
Abu Bakr's hand.

The Prophetﷺ was buried in Aisha's house and
that became his grave.

To him we send peace and blessings, the one whose
name is most praised.

54   *Al Imran, verse 144, Al Qur'an*

REFERENCE

1   *Ibrahim, verse 37, Al Qur'an*

2   *Al Baqara, verse 128, Al Qur'an*

3   *Al Baqara, verse 129, Al Qur'an*

4   *Ibn Hisham,Sahih Muslim & Jami' Al Tirmizi book of virtues*

5   *Al Baqara, verse 127, Al Qur'an*

6   *Al Fil, Al Qur'an*

7   *Al Quraish, Al Qur'an*

8   *Ibn Hisham, vol.1 page 120. 2006 Darul Hadith, Cairo*

9   *Ibn Hisham, vol.1 page 123. 2006 Darul Hadith, Cairo*

10   *Sahih Muslim, book of faith & Ibn Hisham*

11   *Sahih Al Bukhari, book of hiring*

12   *Jami' Al Tirmizi book of virtues*

13   *Ibn Hisham, vol.1 page 141. 2006 Darul Hadith, Cairo*

14   *Ibn Hisham, vol.1 page 144. 2006 Darul Hadith, Cairo*

15   *Ibn Hisham, vol.1 page 146. 2006 Darul Hadith, Cairo*

16   *Adab Al Mufrad, book of behaviour*

17   *Sahih Al Bukhari, book of revelation*

18   *Al Alaq, verses 1-5, Al Qur'an*

19   *Sahih Al Bukhari, book of revelation*

20   *Ibn Hisham, vol.1 page 178. 2006 Darul Hadith, Cairo*

21   *Sahih Muslim, book of faith*

22   *Al Masad, verse 1, Al Qur'an*

23   *Ibn Hisham, vol.1 page 206. 2006 Darul Hadith, Cairo*

24   *Ibn Hisham, vol.1 page 227. 2006 Darul Hadith, Cairo*

25   *Ibn Hisham, vol 1 page 261. 2006 Darul Hadith, Cairo*

26   *A Bukhari, book of beginning of creation*

27   *Al Jinn, verses 1-2 & Al Ahqaf verses 29-31, Al Qur'an*

28   *Al Isra', verse 1, Al Qur'an*

29   *Ibn Hisham, vol.1 page 285. 2006 Darul Hadith, Cairo*

30   *Referred to in Al Najm, verses 8-18, Al Qur'an*

31   *Al Bukhari, book of beginning of creation*

32   *Ibn Hisham, vol.1 page 287. 2006 Darul Hadith, Cairo*

33   *Ibn Hisham, vol.1 page 313. 2006 Darul Hadith, Cairo*

34   *Ibn Hisham, vol.1 page 352. 2006 Darul Hadith, Cairo*

35   *Al Tawba, verse 40, Al Qur'an*

36   *Zad al Ma'ad, vol 2, page 50. 2005 Resalah Publishers, Beirut*

37   *Ibn Hisham, vol.1 page 364. 2006 Darul Hadith, Cairo*

38   *Sahih Al Bukhari, book of patients*

39   *Al Haj, verses 39-40 Al Qur'an*

40   *Ibn Hisham, vol.1 page 458. 2006 Darul Hadith, Cairo*

41   *Al Anfal, verse 8, Al Qur'an*

42   *Sahih Al Bukhari, book of Jihad*

43   *Jami' Al Tirmizi book of Tafsir*

44   *Deuteronomy 20.11 to 20.15 - The Bible*

45   *Al Nur, verses 11 & 12, Al Qur'an*

46   *Al Fath, verses 18 & 19, Al Qur'an*

47   *Sahih Al Bukhari, book of Tafseer*

48   *Sahih Al Bukhari, book of Maghazi*

49   *Sahih Muslim, book of Jihad & Expeditions*

50   *Al Tawba, verse 25 7 26, Al Qur'an*

51   *Sahih Al Bukhari, Book of Maghazi,*

52   *Sunan ibn Majah, book of Rituals*

53   *Al Ma'idah, verse 3, Al Qur'an*

54   *Al Imran, verse 144, Al Qur'an*

Notes

Notes

SLEEPING
LIKE THE
PROPHET ﷺ
40 PROPHETIC TRADITIONS IN RHYMING ENGLISH

WRITTEN BY MOIN UDDIN KHAN
ILLUSTRATED BY KAMRUL HUSSAIN

WALKING
LIKE THE
PROPHET ﷺ

40 PROPHETIC TRADITIONS IN RHYMING ENGLISH

WRITTEN BY MOIN UDDIN KHAN
ILLUSTRATED BY KAMRUL HUSSAIN

About SHADE

SHADE is a UK based charitable umbrella organisation, which endeavours to help society tackle many of the challenges it faces. SHADE runs various projects and activities for the community at large, its programmes engage people from all walks of life and brings them together to encourage respect, understanding and tolerance. It has five different sectors in which there are projects dealing with different aspects of an individual's needs. This has been divided into five sectors: Social, Health, Aid, Development & Education.

Support Us

Visit: www.alrawda.org/donate

Phone: 020 7998 7768

Bank Transfer:
HSBC Bank
a/c: 12030748
s/c: 40-02-34

UK Charity No. 1149699

The Shade Centre
Unit 1, Church Rd Studios
62 Church Road, London E12 6AF
W: www.theshade.org | E: info@theshade.org